Study Habits and Hints

What are some things that you need to do before you sit down to do your homework?
You can reduce the time you spend on homework and improve your learning, if you do a few simple things:
1. Know what your assignments are. This book will help you to do this.
2. Gather all the materials that you will need to do your assignments (assignment book, textbook, paper, pens and pencils, eraser, etc.).
3. Make sure the place you choose to do your homework is free of distractions.
4. Choose a time to do your homework when you are alert.
5. Plan your time. Start by doing those assignments that are easy and can be done in the shortest amount of time. When these are completed, do the more difficult, longer assignments. Limit the amount of time that you devote to homework. Your teacher will tell you how much time you should spend doing homework.
6. After you have completed an assignment, review it to make sure it is correct. Check your assignment book to make sure you have done the proper assignment. Ask your parents to check your work.
7. Be neat with your work and write clearly. This will save you time while you are doing your work.
8. Do not put off doing homework, otherwise you will only have more to do when you start.

What should you do if you don't know how to do the homework?
1. Usually, your homework is a reinforcement of the work done in school. Therefore, you should know how to do it. If you are unclear about how to do an assignment, you should always ask your teacher. Your teacher wants you to do well and wants to help you. You should never hesitate to ask your teacher how to do something.
2. If you have difficulty doing some work, you should also consult your textbook because it is a silent teacher for you.
3. If you are unable to find help in the textbook, you should ask a friend for help. Look around your classroom and ask yourself: "*Who would be the best person to help me?*" Ask that student if you may call when you have difficulty with homework. Write the student's name and telephone number below.

My homework helper is _____

My homework helper's telephone number is _____

How do I use this book?
At the end of each class or at the end of each day, whenever your teacher gives you your assignments, you should write them in this book. Always check to make sure that you have copied the complete assignment. You should have indicated:
1. The books needed
2. The page number and questions
3. How it is to be done
4. When it is due

In the *Reminders* section, list any important dates that are coming, items that are due at school that week, meetings to attend, TV shows your teachers want you to watch, and any other items.

In the *Note from Parent to Teacher* section, your parent may wish to say something to your teacher or your parent may respond to a note from the teacher. When this happens, show your assignment book to your teacher the next day.

In the *Note from Teacher to Parent* section, your teacher may need to say something to your parent or to respond to a question your parent asked. You should show this to your parent that evening.

Students and Catholic Social Teaching

"The Church's social teaching is a rich treasure of wisdom about building a just society and living lives of holiness amidst the challenges of modern society. Modern Catholic social teaching has been articulated through a tradition of papal, conciliar, and episcopal documents. The depth and richness of this tradition can be understood best through a direct reading of these documents. In these brief reflections, we wish to highlight several of the key themes that are at the heart of our Catholic social tradition."[1]

In the Introduction to *From the Ground Up* (NCEA, 1999), it states: "Over the past several decades, Catholic educators in the United States have responded in a variety of ways to the increasing urgent calls of the church to make its social teaching integral to Catholic education at every level." (p. v)[2]

"The purpose of this process (the assessment of how well Catholic social teaching has been integrated into Catholic education) is to enable the faculty and students to better know, understand, and live the concepts and principals that enliven the sever themes of Catholic social teaching." "Rather, these theories are a framework for action that will take Catholic social teaching into the marketplace, the public square, family life, and all community life." (p. v)[3]

The seven Themes of Catholic Social Teaching are:
1. Life and Dignity of the Human Person *(p. 25)
2. Call to Family, Community, and Participation *(p. 35)
3. Rights and Responsibilities of the Human Person *(p. 45)
4. Option for the Poor and Vulnerable *(p. 55)
5. Dignity of Work and the Rights of Workers *(p. 65)
6. Solidarity of the Human Family *(p. 75)
7. Care for God's Creation *(p. 95)

*Indicates the page on which the theme is quoted in the *Teacher Assignment Book: Teacher As Minister* (Washington, D.C., NCEA, 2004).

In an effort to help students become more aware of these teachings, the Outcome Statement and the Rationale were taken *From the Ground Up* for each grade level and added to the *Catholic School Student Assignment Book*. While only the Outcomes Statement and the Rationale for each grade level have been included here, teachers are encouraged to use the Student Behavioral Objectives and Sample Activities for each grade level included in the book *From the Ground Up* in order to make the Outcomes Statement practical and helpful for students.

Bro. William J. Campbell, S.M., Ed.D.
Associate Executive Director
Department of Elementary Schools
NCEA

Footnotes
1   (http://usccb.org/sdwp/projects/socialteaching/excerpt.htm
2   *From the Ground Up: Teaching Catholic Social Principals in Elementary School*. NCEA, Washington, D.C., 1999.
3   Ibid.

Theme: Life and Dignity of the Human Person

Grade Level:	K
Outcomes Statement:	I know that that every person is loved by God and deserves to be treated with kindness.
Rationale:	Jesus taught us to love others as he loves us.

Grade Level:	1
Outcomes Statement:	I will demonstrate an appreciation for the role of work in my life by using and sharing God-given talents with others.
Rationale:	In our uniqueness, we use our God-given talents in our service toward others. We then learn to appreciate the work of others

Grade Level:	2
Outcomes Statement:	I will acknowledge and respect the good qualities and talents of others.
Rationale:	Because all persons are created by God, we are called to respect and value the uniqueness of ourselves and others.

Grade Level:	3
Outcomes Statement:	I show respect to others.
Rationale:	Every human person is created by God and is therefore valuable and worthy of our respect.

Grade Level:	4
Outcomes Statement:	I will act responsibly to help and defend the basic rights of others.
Rationale:	I realize that respect is necessary for every person because Jesus is in him and her.

Grade Level:	5
Outcomes Statement:	I will help others and defend their rights.
Rationale:	People have dignity and are more important than things.

Grade Level:	6
Outcomes Statement:	I will manifest respect for human life and dignity at every stage of development.
Rationale:	Each person possesses the dignity that comes from God, not from any human quality or accomplishment.

Grade Level:	7
Outcomes Statement:	I try to find positive qualities in people who are different from me.
Rationale:	Life is a gift from God, and includes all creation. As followers of Jesus, we are called to act compassionately.

Grade Level:	8
Outcomes Statement:	I will try to find positive qualities in people who are different from me.
Rationale:	As Christians, we are called by Jesus to act with tolerance and respect.

Theme: Call to Family, Community, and Participation

Grade Level:	K
Outcomes Statement:	I am aware that I have a responsibility to participate in my family life.
Rationale:	For a child to move gradually into a life of Christian service, he or she should have an increasing awareness of family and its relation to the community.
Grade Level:	1
Outcomes Statement:	I understand that I am an important working member of my family, school, parish, and community.
Rationale:	We are called to participate and contribute to the well-being of our families, parishes, and communities.
Grade Level:	2
Outcomes Statement:	I realize that I am called to contribute to society.
Rationale:	For a child to move gradually into a life of Christian service, he or she should have an increasing awareness of the importance of participating in family and community life.
Grade Level:	3
Outcomes Statement:	I recognize the importance of and am committed to exercising responsible membership in my family and community.
Rationale:	For a child to move gradually into a life of Christian service, he or she should have an increasing awareness of family and its relationship to the community.
Grade Level:	4
Outcomes Statement:	I recognize the importance of and am committed to membership in family and community.
Rationale:	For a child to move gradually into a life of Christian service, he or she should have an increasing awareness of the importance of participating in family and community life.
Grade Level:	5
Outcomes Statement:	I recognize the importance of and am committed to exercising responsible membership in the family and community as well as becoming more aware of community involvement.
Rationale:	Family is the basic unit of society. We have the responsibility to be involved in the community, our larger family
Grade Level:	6
Outcomes Statement:	I am committed to taking positive steps to build up family life at home and to be a participating member of the community.
Rationale:	The family is the basic unit where we learn and act on our values. We have the right and responsibility to participate in and contribute to the diverse communities in society.
Grade Level:	7
Outcomes Statement:	I find positive qualities in people who are different from me.
Rationale:	Life is a gift from God and includes all creation. As followers of Jesus, we are called to act compassionately.
Grade Level:	8
Outcomes Statement:	I recognizes the importance of and am committed to exercising membership in the family and community.
Rationale:	The family is the basic unit of society. We have the responsibility to be involved in the community, our larger family.

Theme: Rights and Responsibilities of the Human Person

Grade Level:	K
Outcomes Statement:	I am willing to work with others, to cooperate and share.
Rationale:	Christians are called to treat each other and resolve their conflicts in ways consistent with Jesus' teaching and example.
Grade Level:	1
Outcomes Statement:	I am willing to work hard both individually and as a member of a group, with tolerance and respect toward others.
Rationale:	The Church asks that we work both individually and together to create a harmonious group setting with tolerance and respect for all.
Grade Level:	2
Outcomes Statement:	I understand the term "*human rights*" and the responsibilities that go along with these rights.
Rationale:	Christians are called to treat each other and resolve conflicts in ways consistent with Jesus' teaching and example.
Grade Level:	3
Outcomes Statement:	I understand what is included in the term "*human rights*" and know the responsibilities that go along with them.
Rationale:	The basic rights of humans include: the rights to freedom of conscience and religious liberty, to raise a family, to immigrate, to live free from unfair discrimination, and to have earthly goods sufficient for oneself and one's family.
Grade Level:	4
Outcomes Statement:	I understand the basic concept of "*human rights.*"
Rationale:	We understand that we are to care for all living things and respect the rights of others.
Grade Level:	5
Outcomes Statement:	I understand the basic concept of "*human rights.*"
Rationale:	We have responsibility to respect the rights of one another.
Grade Level:	6
Outcomes Statement:	I understand the basic concept of "*human rights.*"
Rationale:	People have an obligation to respect the rights of others and to work for the common good.
Grade Level:	7
Outcomes Statement:	I am willing to defend the human rights of others when they are threatened.
Rationale:	As followers of Jesus, we are Church, the Body of Christ, and thus we are called to reach out with Christ to those who suffer.
Grade Level:	8
Outcomes Statement:	I am committed to advancing the common good in society.
Rationale:	Our Church, the community of Jesus, is called to be a community of compassion.

Theme: Option for the Poor and Vulnerable

Grade Level:	K
Outcomes Statement:	I will become aware that some children are poor and that I should try to help them.
Rationale:	Christians are called to respond to the needs of Christ's people, especially the poor and needy.
Grade Level:	1
Outcomes Statement:	I will reach out to children who have less than I have.
Rationale:	God blesses those who come to the aid of the poor. Love for the poor is an integral part of living a true Christian life.
Grade Level:	2
Outcomes Statement:	I am aware of the need to share personal resources with the poor and needy.
Rationale:	Christians are called to respond to the needs of Christ's people, especially the poor and needy.
Grade Level:	3
Outcomes Statement:	I am committed to sharing personal resources to help the poor.
Rationale:	The Church appeals to everyone to recognize a special obligation to the poor and vulnerable, to defend and promote their dignity, and to ensure that they can participate fully in society.
Grade Level:	4
Outcomes Statement:	I will participate in service and advocacy projects to help persons who are less fortunate.
Rationale:	We follow Jesus' second Great Commandment by loving others as we love ourselves and by sharing our resources with others.
Grade Level:	5
Outcomes Statement:	I will consider the primary needs of others before my secondary needs.
Rationale:	We need to contribute from our own resources to ensure that all have the basic requirements for life with dignity.
Grade Level:	6
Outcomes Statement:	I will consider needs of others before my own secondary needs.
Rationale:	As Christians, we are called to respond to the needs of our brothers and sisters.
Grade Level:	7
Outcomes Statement:	I will work to lessen poverty by empowering people to end their dependency on others.
Rationale:	As followers of Jesus, we are called to develop and enhance the skills of the less fortunate.
Grade Level:	8
Outcomes Statement:	I will work to lessen poverty by empowering people to end their dependency.
Rationale:	As Christians, we put the needs of the poor first.

Theme: Dignity of Work and the Rights of Workers

Grade Level:	K
Outcomes Statement:	I will demonstrate an appreciation for the role of work in my life by using and sharing God-given talents with others.
Rationale:	In our uniqueness, we use our God-given talents in our service toward others. We then learn to appreciate the work of others.

Grade Level:	1
Outcomes Statement:	All aspects of a good life involve work.
Rationale:	Work is positive and something to be proud of. Everyone should be able to provide for his or her life and that of his or her family as well as serve the community.

Grade Level:	2
Outcomes Statement:	I understand that work affects me in a positive way and is an expression of my human self-worth.
Rationale:	All people should put their best effort into their work and accept and appreciate the work of others.

Grade Level:	3
Outcomes Statement:	I will put my best efforts into my work.
Rationale:	Work is more than a way to make a living. It is an expression of human dignity and a form of continuing participation in God's creation.

Grade Level:	4
Outcomes Statement:	I will exercise responsibility for the gifts and talents God has given me.
Rationale:	Work is more than a way to make a living. It is an expression of human dignity and a form of continuing participation in God's creation.

Grade Level:	5
Outcomes Statement:	I will demonstrate an appreciation of work and recognize every worker's contributions to society.
Rationale:	Work is a way for us to participate in God's creation.

Grade Level:	6
Outcomes Statement:	I will give my best at work and make a commitment to contribute to society by means of that work.
Rationale:	Work is an expression of human dignity, and people have the right to decent and productive work.

Grade Level:	7
Outcomes Statement:	I recognize my talents and will put them to good use.
Rationale:	By virtue of baptism, every Christian is called to service and this call is fulfilled through a variety of ministries.

Grade Level:	8
Outcomes Statement:	I will appreciate my talents and those of others and work toward ensuring the free use of these talents in the workplace and beyond.
Rationale:	By virtue of baptism, every Christian is called to service and this call is fulfilled through a variety of ministries.

Theme: Solidarity of the Human Family

Grade Level:	K
Outcomes Statement:	I will become aware of traditions in other cultures that are the same and different, i.e., language, etc.
Rationale:	We are one human family.
Grade Level:	1
Outcomes Statement:	I will become aware of responsibilities to others throughout the world.
Rationale:	In a linked and limited world, our responsibilities to one another cross national and other boundaries.
Grade Level:	2
Outcomes Statement:	I will try understand and accept all people through awareness of others' customs and cultures.
Rationale:	God's plan is for us to live in harmony with all people, cultures, and customs.
Grade Level:	3
Outcomes Statement:	I will try to understand the commitment to the common good and be committed to work for world peace.
Rationale:	Violent conflict and the violation of the dignity and rights of people anywhere on the globe diminish each of us. Solidarity expresses the church's concern for world peace, global development, environment, and international human rights.
Grade Level:	4
Outcomes Statement:	I am aware of responsibilities to others around the earth.
Rationale:	God's plan is for us to live in harmony with all people, cultures, and customs.
Grade Level:	5
Outcomes Statement:	I will become aware of responsibilities to others throughout the world.
Rationale:	We are one people created by God and are called to carry one another's burdens.
Grade Level:	6
Outcomes Statement:	I will be committed to work for world peace and global development.
Rationale:	Since we are one human family, our responsibilities to one another cross national, social, ethnic, and economic boundaries. The denial of dignity and rights to people anywhere on the globe diminishes each of us.
Grade Level:	7
Outcomes Statement:	I am willing to contribute to global development according to my personal talents.
Rationale:	"For just as the body is one and has many members, and all the members of the body, though many, are one body, so it is with Christ." (1 Cor. 12:12-26)
Grade Level:	8
Outcomes Statement:	I am committed to world peace.
Rationale:	"For just as the body is one and has many members, and all the members of the body, though many, are one body, so it is with Christ." (1 Cor. 12:12-26)

Theme: Care for God's Creation

Grade Level:	K
Outcomes Statement:	I will learn that part of God's plan is for me to live in harmony with my classmates and nature.
Rationale:	We are all called to be keepers of the earth.
Grade Level:	1
Outcomes Statement:	I will learn that God wants us to take care of all of God's creation.
Rationale:	God entrusted us to be caretakers of the created world and to preserve its beauty.
Grade Level:	2
Outcomes Statement:	I will learn that God wants us to take care of his creation.
Rationale:	God gave us our beautiful world and wants us to care for it.
Grade Level:	3
Outcomes Statement:	I know that God wants us to take care of all of his creation.
Rationale:	God entrusted us to take care of the earth.
Grade Level:	4
Outcomes Statement:	I know that God wants us to take care of all of his creation.
Rationale:	God entrusted us to be caretakers of the created world and to preserve it.
Grade Level:	5
Outcomes Statement:	I know that God wants us to care for all of his creation.
Rationale:	God has given us this world and we must preserve its beauty and resources.
Grade Level:	6
Outcomes Statement:	I know that God wants us to take care of all of his creation.
Rationale:	God entrusted us to be caretakers of the created world and to preserve it for future generations.
Grade Level:	7
Outcomes Statement:	I recognize the importance of caring for creation and will participate in activities to promote stewardship of the earth.
Rationale:	God has entrusted the world to us as caretakers of God's creation.
Grade Level:	8
Outcomes Statement:	I am willing to contribute to global development according to my personal talents.
Rationale:	God has entrusted the world to us as caretakers of God's creation.

ASSIGNMENTS

Assignments for the week of : Due Date

MONDAY
- Religion
- Reading
- Science
- Math
- Social Studies
- Language Arts/ English

TUESDAY
- Religion
- Reading
- Science
- Math
- Social Studies
- Language Arts/ English

WEDNESDAY
- Religion
- Reading
- Science
- Math
- Social Studies
- Language Arts/ English

Word of the week :

		Due Date
Religion		**THURSDAY**
Reading		
Science		
Math		
Social Studies		
Language Arts/ English		
Religion		**FRIDAY**
Reading		
Science		
Math		
Social Studies		
Language Arts/ English		

Reminders:

1. _____
2. _____
3. _____

Note from parent to teacher _____

Note from teacher to parent _____

✢ *Jesus, help me to do my work well.*

	Assignments for the week of :	Due Date
MONDAY	Religion	
	Reading	
	Science	
	Math	
	Social Studies	
	Language Arts/ English	
TUESDAY	Religion	
	Reading	
	Science	
	Math	
	Social Studies	
	Language Arts/ English	
WEDNESDAY	Religion	
	Reading	
	Science	
	Math	
	Social Studies	
	Language Arts/ English	

Word of the week :

Due Date

	THURSDAY
Religion	
Reading	
Science	
Math	
Social Studies	
Language Arts/ English	

	FRIDAY
Religion	
Reading	
Science	
Math	
Social Studies	
Language Arts/ English	

Reminders:

1. ___
2. ___
3. ___

Note from parent to teacher ___

Note from teacher to parent ___

✛ *Spirit of Truth, help me pay attention in school.*

Assignments for the week of :   Due Date

MONDAY
- Religion
- Reading
- Science
- Math
- Social Studies
- Language Arts/ English

TUESDAY
- Religion
- Reading
- Science
- Math
- Social Studies
- Language Arts/ English

WEDNESDAY
- Religion
- Reading
- Science
- Math
- Social Studies
- Language Arts/ English

Word of the week :

		Due Date
Religion		**THURSDAY**
Reading		
Science		
Math		
Social Studies		
Language Arts/ English		
Religion		**FRIDAY**
Reading		
Science		
Math		
Social Studies		
Language Arts/ English		

Reminders:

1. _____
2. _____
3. _____

Note from parent to teacher _____
_____
_____

Note from teacher to parent _____
_____

✜ *Mary, ask your Son, Jesus, to help me with my tests.*

	Assignments for the week of :	Due Date
MONDAY	Religion	
	Reading	
	Science	
	Math	
	Social Studies	
	Language Arts/ English	
TUESDAY	Religion	
	Reading	
	Science	
	Math	
	Social Studies	
	Language Arts/ English	
WEDNESDAY	Religion	
	Reading	
	Science	
	Math	
	Social Studies	
	Language Arts/ English	

Word of the week : | Due Date

		THURSDAY
Religion		
Reading		
Science		
Math		
Social Studies		
Language Arts/ English		

		FRIDAY
Religion		
Reading		
Science		
Math		
Social Studies		
Language Arts/ English		

Reminders:

1. _____
2. _____
3. _____

Note from parent to teacher _____
_____
_____

Note from teacher to parent _____

✢ *Thank you, God, for all Your help.*

Assignments for the week of :

Due Date

MONDAY
- Religion
- Reading
- Science
- Math
- Social Studies
- Language Arts/English

TUESDAY
- Religion
- Reading
- Science
- Math
- Social Studies
- Language Arts/English

WEDNESDAY
- Religion
- Reading
- Science
- Math
- Social Studies
- Language Arts/English

Due Date

Word of the week : Due Date

	THURSDAY
Religion	
Reading	
Science	
Math	
Social Studies	
Language Arts/ English	

	FRIDAY
Religion	
Reading	
Science	
Math	
Social Studies	
Language Arts/ English	

Reminders:

1. _____
2. _____
3. _____

Note from parent to teacher _____

Note from teacher to parent _____

✙ *Since I love You, Jesus, I will study carefully.*

21

Assignments for the week of :

Due Date

MONDAY
- Religion
- Reading
- Science
- Math
- Social Studies
- Language Arts/ English

TUESDAY
- Religion
- Reading
- Science
- Math
- Social Studies
- Language Arts/ English

WEDNESDAY
- Religion
- Reading
- Science
- Math
- Social Studies
- Language Arts/ English

		Due Date
Word of the week:		

THURSDAY

Religion	
Reading	
Science	
Math	
Social Studies	
Language Arts/ English	

FRIDAY

Religion	
Reading	
Science	
Math	
Social Studies	
Language Arts/ English	

Reminders:

1. _____
2. _____
3. _____

Note from parent to teacher _____
_____
_____

Note from teacher to parent _____
_____

✧ *Please help me to do my homework quickly.*

Assignments for the week of : Due Date

MONDAY

- Religion
- Reading
- Science
- Math
- Social Studies
- Language Arts/ English

TUESDAY

- Religion
- Reading
- Science
- Math
- Social Studies
- Language Arts/ English

WEDNESDAY

- Religion
- Reading
- Science
- Math
- Social Studies
- Language Arts/ English

Word of the week :

Due Date

	THURSDAY
Religion	
Reading	
Science	
Math	
Social Studies	
Language Arts/ English	

	FRIDAY
Religion	
Reading	
Science	
Math	
Social Studies	
Language Arts/ English	

Reminders:

1. _____
2. _____
3. _____

Note from parent to teacher _____
_____
_____

Note from teacher to parent _____
_____

✚ *Father in heaven, I need Your help now.*

25

		Assignments for the week of :	Due Date
MONDAY	Religion		
	Reading		
	Science		
	Math		
	Social Studies		
	Language Arts/ English		
TUESDAY	Religion		
	Reading		
	Science		
	Math		
	Social Studies		
	Language Arts/ English		
WEDNESDAY	Religion		
	Reading		
	Science		
	Math		
	Social Studies		
	Language Arts/ English		

Word of the week :

		Due Date
Religion		
Reading		
Science		
Math		
Social Studies		
Language Arts/ English		
Religion		
Reading		
Science		
Math		
Social Studies		
Language Arts/ English		

THURSDAY

FRIDAY

Reminders:

1. _____
2. _____
3. _____

Note from parent to teacher _____

Note from teacher to parent _____

✜ *Holy Spirit, help me to study hard for my test.*

Assignments for the week of :   **Due Date**

MONDAY
- Religion
- Reading
- Science
- Math
- Social Studies
- Language Arts/ English

TUESDAY
- Religion
- Reading
- Science
- Math
- Social Studies
- Language Arts/ English

WEDNESDAY
- Religion
- Reading
- Science
- Math
- Social Studies
- Language Arts/ English

Word of the week :

Due Date

	THURSDAY
Religion	
Reading	
Science	
Math	
Social Studies	
Language Arts/ English	

	FRIDAY
Religion	
Reading	
Science	
Math	
Social Studies	
Language Arts/ English	

Reminders:

1. _____

2. _____

3. _____

Note from parent to teacher _____
_____
_____

Note from teacher to parent _____

✛ Mother Cabrini, you loved all children. Pray for me.

Assignments for the week of :   **Due Date**

MONDAY

Religion	
Reading	
Science	
Math	
Social Studies	
Language Arts/ English	

TUESDAY

Religion	
Reading	
Science	
Math	
Social Studies	
Language Arts/ English	

WEDNESDAY

Religion	
Reading	
Science	
Math	
Social Studies	
Language Arts/ English	

Word of the week :

Due Date

	THURSDAY
Religion	
Reading	
Science	
Math	
Social Studies	
Language Arts/ English	

	FRIDAY
Religion	
Reading	
Science	
Math	
Social Studies	
Language Arts/ English	

Reminders:

1. _____
2. _____
3. _____

Note from parent to teacher _____

Note from teacher to parent _____

✞ *Jesus, I'm thinking about a lot of things. Help me pay attention.*

31

Assignments for the week of :   Due Date

MONDAY

- Religion
- Reading
- Science
- Math
- Social Studies
- Language Arts/ English

TUESDAY

- Religion
- Reading
- Science
- Math
- Social Studies
- Language Arts/ English

WEDNESDAY

- Religion
- Reading
- Science
- Math
- Social Studies
- Language Arts/ English

Word of the week :

		Due Date
Religion		
Reading		
Science		
Math		
Social Studies		
Language Arts/ English		

THURSDAY

Religion		
Reading		
Science		
Math		
Social Studies		
Language Arts/ English		

FRIDAY

Reminders:

1. _____
2. _____
3. _____

Note from parent to teacher _____

Note from teacher to parent _____

✢ *Dear God, I know I can do this with your help.*

		Due Date
Assignments for the week of :		
MONDAY		
Religion		
Reading		
Science		
Math		
Social Studies		
Language Arts/ English		
TUESDAY		
Religion		
Reading		
Science		
Math		
Social Studies		
Language Arts/ English		
WEDNESDAY		
Religion		
Reading		
Science		
Math		
Social Studies		
Language Arts/ English		

Word of the week :   Due Date

Religion		**THURSDAY**
Reading		
Science		
Math		
Social Studies		
Language Arts/ English		
Religion		**FRIDAY**
Reading		
Science		
Math		
Social Studies		
Language Arts/ English		

Reminders:

1. _____
2. _____
3. _____

Note from parent to teacher _____
_____
_____

Note from teacher to parent _____
_____

✢ *Jesus, help me to remember everything I need for school.*

Assignments for the week of :   Due Date

MONDAY
- Religion
- Reading
- Science
- Math
- Social Studies
- Language Arts/ English

TUESDAY
- Religion
- Reading
- Science
- Math
- Social Studies
- Language Arts/ English

WEDNESDAY
- Religion
- Reading
- Science
- Math
- Social Studies
- Language Arts/ English

Word of the week :

		Due Date
Religion		**THURSDAY**
Reading		
Science		
Math		
Social Studies		
Language Arts/ English		
Religion		**FRIDAY**
Reading		
Science		
Math		
Social Studies		
Language Arts/ English		

Reminders:

1. _____
2. _____
3. _____

Note from parent to teacher _____
_____
_____

Note from teacher to parent _____
_____

✛ *St. Joseph, you helped Your Son, Jesus. Help me now.*

Assignments for the week of :   Due Date

MONDAY
- Religion
- Reading
- Science
- Math
- Social Studies
- Language Arts/ English

TUESDAY
- Religion
- Reading
- Science
- Math
- Social Studies
- Language Arts/ English

WEDNESDAY
- Religion
- Reading
- Science
- Math
- Social Studies
- Language Arts/ English

Word of the week :

		Due Date
Religion		
Reading		
Science		**THURSDAY**
Math		
Social Studies		
Language Arts/ English		
Religion		
Reading		
Science		**FRIDAY**
Math		
Social Studies		
Language Arts/ English		

Reminders:

1. _____
2. _____
3. _____

Note from parent to teacher _____
_____
_____
_____

Note from teacher to parent _____
_____
_____

✢ *Jesus, I know I please You and help myself when I work hard.*

Assignments for the week of :   **Due Date**

MONDAY

- **Religion**
- **Reading**
- **Science**
- **Math**
- **Social Studies**
- **Language Arts/ English**

TUESDAY

- **Religion**
- **Reading**
- **Science**
- **Math**
- **Social Studies**
- **Language Arts/ English**

WEDNESDAY

- **Religion**
- **Reading**
- **Science**
- **Math**
- **Social Studies**
- **Language Arts/ English**

Word of the week :

		Due Date
Religion		
Reading		
Science		**THURSDAY**
Math		
Social Studies		
Language Arts/ English		
Religion		
Reading		
Science		**FRIDAY**
Math		
Social Studies		
Language Arts/ English		

Reminders:

1. _____
2. _____
3. _____

Note from parent to teacher _____
_____
_____

Note from teacher to parent _____
_____

✢ *Dear Guardian Angel, keep me attentive to what I must do.*

Assignments for the week of :   Due Date

MONDAY

Religion		
Reading		
Science		
Math		
Social Studies		
Language Arts/ English		

TUESDAY

Religion		
Reading		
Science		
Math		
Social Studies		
Language Arts/ English		

WEDNESDAY

Religion		
Reading		
Science		
Math		
Social Studies		
Language Arts/ English		

Word of the week :

		Due Date
Religion		**THURSDAY**
Reading		
Science		
Math		
Social Studies		
Language Arts/ English		
Religion		**FRIDAY**
Reading		
Science		
Math		
Social Studies		
Language Arts/ English		

Reminders:

1. _____

2. _____

3. _____

Note from parent to teacher _____

Note from teacher to parent _____

✚ *Jesus, help me to do well on this big test.*

Assignments for the week of :   **Due Date**

MONDAY

- Religion
- Reading
- Science
- Math
- Social Studies
- Language Arts/ English

TUESDAY

- Religion
- Reading
- Science
- Math
- Social Studies
- Language Arts/ English

WEDNESDAY

- Religion
- Reading
- Science
- Math
- Social Studies
- Language Arts/ English

Word of the week :

Due Date

	THURSDAY
Religion	
Reading	
Science	
Math	
Social Studies	
Language Arts/ English	

	FRIDAY
Religion	
Reading	
Science	
Math	
Social Studies	
Language Arts/ English	

Reminders:

1. _____
2. _____
3. _____

Note from parent to teacher _____

Note from teacher to parent _____

✚ *Jesus, help me to remember to thank my teachers.*

Assignments for the week of :   Due Date

MONDAY
- Religion
- Reading
- Science
- Math
- Social Studies
- Language Arts/ English

TUESDAY
- Religion
- Reading
- Science
- Math
- Social Studies
- Language Arts/ English

WEDNESDAY
- Religion
- Reading
- Science
- Math
- Social Studies
- Language Arts/ English

Word of the week :

Due Date

Religion		**THURSDAY**
Reading		
Science		
Math		
Social Studies		
Language Arts/ English		

Religion		**FRIDAY**
Reading		
Science		
Math		
Social Studies		
Language Arts/ English		

Reminders:

1. _____

2. _____

3. _____

Note from parent to teacher _____
_____
_____

Note from teacher to parent _____
_____

✠ *Jesus, I know you are here to help me.*

		Assignments for the week of :	Due Date
MONDAY	Religion		
	Reading		
	Science		
	Math		
	Social Studies		
	Language Arts/ English		
TUESDAY	Religion		
	Reading		
	Science		
	Math		
	Social Studies		
	Language Arts/ English		
WEDNESDAY	Religion		
	Reading		
	Science		
	Math		
	Social Studies		
	Language Arts/ English		

Word of the week :

		Due Date	
Religion			**T H U R S D A Y**
Reading			
Science			
Math			
Social Studies			
Language Arts/ English			
Religion			**F R I D A Y**
Reading			
Science			
Math			
Social Studies			
Language Arts/ English			

Reminders:

1. _____

2. _____

3. _____

Note from parent to teacher _____

_____

_____

Note from teacher to parent _____

_____

_____

✤ *Mary, Seat of Wisdom, pray for me.*

Assignments for the week of : Due Date

MONDAY
- Religion
- Reading
- Science
- Math
- Social Studies
- Language Arts/English

TUESDAY
- Religion
- Reading
- Science
- Math
- Social Studies
- Language Arts/English

WEDNESDAY
- Religion
- Reading
- Science
- Math
- Social Studies
- Language Arts/English

Word of the week:

		Due Date
Religion		**T**
Reading		**H**
Science		**U**
Math		**R**
Social Studies		**S**
Language Arts/ English		**D**
		A
		Y
Religion		
Reading		**F**
Science		**R**
Math		**I**
Social Studies		**D**
Language Arts/ English		**A**
		Y

Reminders:

1. _____
2. _____
3. _____

Note from parent to teacher _____
_____
_____

Note from teacher to parent _____
_____

✚ *Jesus, I need you now.*

Assignments for the week of :   **Due Date**

MONDAY

- Religion
- Reading
- Science
- Math
- Social Studies
- Language Arts/ English

TUESDAY

- Religion
- Reading
- Science
- Math
- Social Studies
- Language Arts/ English

WEDNESDAY

- Religion
- Reading
- Science
- Math
- Social Studies
- Language Arts/ English

Word of the week :   Due Date

Religion		**T H U R S D A Y**
Reading		
Science		
Math		
Social Studies		
Language Arts/ English		
Religion		**F R I D A Y**
Reading		
Science		
Math		
Social Studies		
Language Arts/ English		

Reminders:

1. _____
2. _____
3. _____

Note from parent to teacher _____
_____
_____

Note from teacher to parent _____
_____

✜ *Jesus, I appreciate Your help.*

Assignments for the week of: Due Date

MONDAY
- Religion
- Reading
- Science
- Math
- Social Studies
- Language Arts/English

TUESDAY
- Religion
- Reading
- Science
- Math
- Social Studies
- Language Arts/English

WEDNESDAY
- Religion
- Reading
- Science
- Math
- Social Studies
- Language Arts/English

Word of the week :

Due Date

	THURSDAY
Religion	
Reading	
Science	
Math	
Social Studies	
Language Arts/ English	

	FRIDAY
Religion	
Reading	
Science	
Math	
Social Studies	
Language Arts/ English	

Reminders:

1. _____

2. _____

3. _____

Note from parent to teacher _____

_____

_____

Note from teacher to parent _____

✢ *Father, open my mind, so I may know You through Your creation.*

		Assignments for the week of :	Due Date
M O N D A Y	Religion		
	Reading		
	Science		
	Math		
	Social Studies		
	Language Arts/ English		
T U E S D A Y	Religion		
	Reading		
	Science		
	Math		
	Social Studies		
	Language Arts/ English		
W E D N E S D A Y	Religion		
	Reading		
	Science		
	Math		
	Social Studies		
	Language Arts/ English		

Word of the week :   Due Date

		THURSDAY
Religion		
Reading		
Science		
Math		
Social Studies		
Language Arts/ English		

		FRIDAY
Religion		
Reading		
Science		
Math		
Social Studies		
Language Arts/ English		

Reminders:

1. _____
2. _____
3. _____

Note from parent to teacher _____
_____
_____

Note from teacher to parent _____
_____

✚ *When I study hard, I follow Your example, Jesus.*

	Assignments for the week of :	Due Date
MONDAY	Religion	
	Reading	
	Science	
	Math	
	Social Studies	
	Language Arts/ English	
TUESDAY	Religion	
	Reading	
	Science	
	Math	
	Social Studies	
	Language Arts/ English	
WEDNESDAY	Religion	
	Reading	
	Science	
	Math	
	Social Studies	
	Language Arts/ English	

Word of the week :		Due Date
Religion		**T H U R S D A Y**
Reading		
Science		
Math		
Social Studies		
Language Arts/ English		
Religion		**F R I D A Y**
Reading		
Science		
Math		
Social Studies		
Language Arts/ English		

Reminders:

1. _____
2. _____
3. _____

Note from parent to teacher _____
_____
_____

Note from teacher to parent _____
_____

✤ *Dear God, help me to remember the correct answers.*

59

Assignments for the week of :   Due Date

MONDAY

- Religion
- Reading
- Science
- Math
- Social Studies
- Language Arts/English

TUESDAY

- Religion
- Reading
- Science
- Math
- Social Studies
- Language Arts/English

WEDNESDAY

- Religion
- Reading
- Science
- Math
- Social Studies
- Language Arts/English

Word of the week :　　　　　　　　　　　　　　　　　　　　　Due Date

Religion		
Reading		
Science		
Math		**THURSDAY**
Social Studies		
Language Arts/ English		
Religion		
Reading		
Science		
Math		**FRIDAY**
Social Studies		
Language Arts/ English		

Reminders:

1. _____

2. _____

3. _____

Note from parent to teacher _____
_____
_____

Note from teacher to parent _____

✙ *Mother Seton, you taught teachers. Teach me now.*

Assignments for the week of :   Due Date

MONDAY
- Religion
- Reading
- Science
- Math
- Social Studies
- Language Arts/English

TUESDAY
- Religion
- Reading
- Science
- Math
- Social Studies
- Language Arts/English

WEDNESDAY
- Religion
- Reading
- Science
- Math
- Social Studies
- Language Arts/English

Word of the week :   Due Date

Religion		**THURSDAY**
Reading		
Science		
Math		
Social Studies		
Language Arts/ English		

Religion		**FRIDAY**
Reading		
Science		
Math		
Social Studies		
Language Arts/ English		

Reminders:

1. _____
2. _____
3. _____

Note from parent to teacher _____

Note from teacher to parent _____

✢ *I don't want to study, but I know I have to. Help me, Jesus.*

Assignments for the week of :   Due Date

MONDAY

- Religion
- Reading
- Science
- Math
- Social Studies
- Language Arts/ English

TUESDAY

- Religion
- Reading
- Science
- Math
- Social Studies
- Language Arts/ English

WEDNESDAY

- Religion
- Reading
- Science
- Math
- Social Studies
- Language Arts/ English

Word of the week :

		Due Date
Religion		**T H U R S D A Y**
Reading		
Science		
Math		
Social Studies		
Language Arts/ English		
Religion		**F R I D A Y**
Reading		
Science		
Math		
Social Studies		
Language Arts/ English		

Reminders:

1. _____
2. _____
3. _____

Note from parent to teacher _____
_____
_____

Note from teacher to parent _____
_____

✜ *Jesus, Light of the World, give me Your Light.*

65

		Assignments for the week of :	Due Date
MONDAY	Religion		
	Reading		
	Science		
	Math		
	Social Studies		
	Language Arts/ English		
TUESDAY	Religion		
	Reading		
	Science		
	Math		
	Social Studies		
	Language Arts/ English		
WEDNESDAY	Religion		
	Reading		
	Science		
	Math		
	Social Studies		
	Language Arts/ English		

Word of the week :

		Due Date
Religion		
Reading		
Science		
Math		**THURSDAY**
Social Studies		
Language Arts/ English		
Religion		
Reading		
Science		**FRIDAY**
Math		
Social Studies		
Language Arts/ English		

Reminders:

1. _____
2. _____
3. _____

Note from parent to teacher _____

Note from teacher to parent _____

✤ *Jesus, the Good Shepherd, take care of me.*

Assignments for the week of :   Due Date

MONDAY

Religion	
Reading	
Science	
Math	
Social Studies	
Language Arts/ English	

TUESDAY

Religion	
Reading	
Science	
Math	
Social Studies	
Language Arts/ English	

WEDNESDAY

Religion	
Reading	
Science	
Math	
Social Studies	
Language Arts/ English	

Word of the week :

Due Date

		THURSDAY
Religion		
Reading		
Science		
Math		
Social Studies		
Language Arts/ English		

		FRIDAY
Religion		
Reading		
Science		
Math		
Social Studies		
Language Arts/ English		

Reminders:

1. _____
2. _____
3. _____

Note from parent to teacher _____

Note from teacher to parent _____

✢ *St. Thomas, you were the doubting apostle. Help me to overcome my doubts.*

		Assignments for the week of :	Due Date
MONDAY	Religion		
	Reading		
	Science		
	Math		
	Social Studies		
	Language Arts/ English		
TUESDAY	Religion		
	Reading		
	Science		
	Math		
	Social Studies		
	Language Arts/ English		
WEDNESDAY	Religion		
	Reading		
	Science		
	Math		
	Social Studies		
	Language Arts/ English		

Word of the week :

		Due Date
Religion		
Reading		
Science		**THURSDAY**
Math		
Social Studies		
Language Arts/ English		

Religion		
Reading		
Science		**FRIDAY**
Math		
Social Studies		
Language Arts/ English		

Reminders:

1. _____
2. _____
3. _____

Note from parent to teacher _____

Note from teacher to parent _____

✢ *My Father, give me knowledge.*

71

Assignments for the week of :   Due Date

MONDAY

- Religion
- Reading
- Science
- Math
- Social Studies
- Language Arts/ English

TUESDAY

- Religion
- Reading
- Science
- Math
- Social Studies
- Language Arts/ English

WEDNESDAY

- Religion
- Reading
- Science
- Math
- Social Studies
- Language Arts/ English

Word of the week :

Due Date

	THURSDAY
Religion	
Reading	
Science	
Math	
Social Studies	
Language Arts/ English	

	FRIDAY
Religion	
Reading	
Science	
Math	
Social Studies	
Language Arts/ English	

Reminders:

1. _____
2. _____
3. _____

Note from parent to teacher _____

Note from teacher to parent _____

✢ *Jesus, thank You for all the help You give me.*

Assignments for the week of :   **Due Date**

MONDAY
- Religion
- Reading
- Science
- Math
- Social Studies
- Language Arts/English

TUESDAY
- Religion
- Reading
- Science
- Math
- Social Studies
- Language Arts/English

WEDNESDAY
- Religion
- Reading
- Science
- Math
- Social Studies
- Language Arts/English

Word of the week :

		Due Date
Religion		
Reading		
Science		**THURSDAY**
Math		
Social Studies		
Language Arts/ English		
Religion		
Reading		
Science		**FRIDAY**
Math		
Social Studies		
Language Arts/ English		

Reminders:

1. _____
2. _____
3. _____

Note from parent to teacher _____

Note from teacher to parent _____

✣ *Holy Mary, Mother of God, pray for me now.*

Assignments for the week of : 　　　　　　　　　　　　　　　　　　　　　　　Due Date

MONDAY
- Religion
- Reading
- Science
- Math
- Social Studies
- Language Arts/English

TUESDAY
- Religion
- Reading
- Science
- Math
- Social Studies
- Language Arts/English

WEDNESDAY
- Religion
- Reading
- Science
- Math
- Social Studies
- Language Arts/English

Word of the week :

		Due Date
Religion		
Reading		**THURSDAY**
Science		
Math		
Social Studies		
Language Arts/ English		

Religion		
Reading		**FRIDAY**
Science		
Math		
Social Studies		
Language Arts/ English		

Reminders:

1. _____

2. _____

3. _____

Note from parent to teacher _____

_____

_____

Note from teacher to parent _____

_____

✤ *Jesus, I am doing my work well because this is what You want.*

77

	Assignments for the week of :	Due Date
MONDAY	Religion	
	Reading	
	Science	
	Math	
	Social Studies	
	Language Arts/ English	
TUESDAY	Religion	
	Reading	
	Science	
	Math	
	Social Studies	
	Language Arts/ English	
WEDNESDAY	Religion	
	Reading	
	Science	
	Math	
	Social Studies	
	Language Arts/ English	

Word of the week :

		Due Date
Religion		
Reading		**THURSDAY**
Science		
Math		
Social Studies		
Language Arts/ English		
Religion		
Reading		**FRIDAY**
Science		
Math		
Social Studies		
Language Arts/ English		

Reminders:

1. _____
2. _____
3. _____

Note from parent to teacher _____
_____
_____

Note from teacher to parent _____
_____

✢ *Jesus, I know I can do it with Your help.*

Assignments for the week of :   Due Date

MONDAY

- Religion
- Reading
- Science
- Math
- Social Studies
- Language Arts/ English

TUESDAY

- Religion
- Reading
- Science
- Math
- Social Studies
- Language Arts/ English

WEDNESDAY

- Religion
- Reading
- Science
- Math
- Social Studies
- Language Arts/ English

Word of the week :   Due Date

	THURSDAY
Religion	
Reading	
Science	
Math	
Social Studies	
Language Arts/ English	

	FRIDAY
Religion	
Reading	
Science	
Math	
Social Studies	
Language Arts/ English	

Reminders:

1. _____
2. _____
3. _____

Note from parent to teacher _____
_____
_____

Note from teacher to parent _____
_____

✦ *My Father, You created the world. Help me with my project.*

81

Assignments for the week of :   Due Date

MONDAY
- Religion
- Reading
- Science
- Math
- Social Studies
- Language Arts/ English

TUESDAY
- Religion
- Reading
- Science
- Math
- Social Studies
- Language Arts/ English

WEDNESDAY
- Religion
- Reading
- Science
- Math
- Social Studies
- Language Arts/ English

Word of the week : 　　　　　　　　　　　　　　　　　　　　　　　　　　　　Due Date

Religion		**THURSDAY**
Reading		
Science		
Math		
Social Studies		
Language Arts/ English		
Religion		**FRIDAY**
Reading		
Science		
Math		
Social Studies		
Language Arts/ English		

Reminders:

1. _____

2. _____

3. _____

Note from parent to teacher _____

_____

_____

Note from teacher to parent _____

_____

✤ *St. John Neumann, you built schools. Help us in this one.*

Assignments for the week of :   Due Date

MONDAY
- Religion
- Reading
- Science
- Math
- Social Studies
- Language Arts/ English

TUESDAY
- Religion
- Reading
- Science
- Math
- Social Studies
- Language Arts/ English

WEDNESDAY
- Religion
- Reading
- Science
- Math
- Social Studies
- Language Arts/ English

Word of the week :

Due Date

THURSDAY

Religion	
Reading	
Science	
Math	
Social Studies	
Language Arts/ English	

FRIDAY

Religion	
Reading	
Science	
Math	
Social Studies	
Language Arts/ English	

Reminders:

1. _____
2. _____
3. _____

Note from parent to teacher _____
_____
_____

Note from teacher to parent _____

✢ *Jesus, I will work hard to thank You for dying for me.*

Assignments for the week of :   Due Date

MONDAY
- Religion
- Reading
- Science
- Math
- Social Studies
- Language Arts/English

TUESDAY
- Religion
- Reading
- Science
- Math
- Social Studies
- Language Arts/English

WEDNESDAY
- Religion
- Reading
- Science
- Math
- Social Studies
- Language Arts/English

Word of the week :

		Due Date
Religion		**THURSDAY**
Reading		
Science		
Math		
Social Studies		
Language Arts/ English		

Religion		**FRIDAY**
Reading		
Science		
Math		
Social Studies		
Language Arts/ English		

Reminders:

1. _____
2. _____
3. _____

Note from parent to teacher _____

Note from teacher to parent _____

✛ *Holy Spirit, give me the wisdom I need now.*

Assignments for the week of :   Due Date

MONDAY

- Religion
- Reading
- Science
- Math
- Social Studies
- Language Arts/ English

TUESDAY

- Religion
- Reading
- Science
- Math
- Social Studies
- Language Arts/ English

WEDNESDAY

- Religion
- Reading
- Science
- Math
- Social Studies
- Language Arts/ English

Word of the week : Due Date

	THURSDAY
Religion	
Reading	
Science	
Math	
Social Studies	
Language Arts/ English	

	FRIDAY
Religion	
Reading	
Science	
Math	
Social Studies	
Language Arts/ English	

Reminders:

1. _____
2. _____
3. _____

Note from parent to teacher _____
_____
_____

Note from teacher to parent _____
_____

✛ *Jesus, stay with me as I study.*

Assignments for the week of :   Due Date

MONDAY

- Religion
- Reading
- Science
- Math
- Social Studies
- Language Arts/ English

TUESDAY

- Religion
- Reading
- Science
- Math
- Social Studies
- Language Arts/ English

WEDNESDAY

- Religion
- Reading
- Science
- Math
- Social Studies
- Language Arts/ English

Word of the week :   Due Date

THURSDAY

- Religion
- Reading
- Science
- Math
- Social Studies
- Language Arts/English

FRIDAY

- Religion
- Reading
- Science
- Math
- Social Studies
- Language Arts/English

Reminders:

1. _____
2. _____
3. _____

Note from parent to teacher _____

Note from teacher to parent _____

✤ *Mary, pray for me as I prepare for my tests.*

91

Assignments for the week of :   Due Date

MONDAY
- Religion
- Reading
- Science
- Math
- Social Studies
- Language Arts/ English

TUESDAY
- Religion
- Reading
- Science
- Math
- Social Studies
- Language Arts/ English

WEDNESDAY
- Religion
- Reading
- Science
- Math
- Social Studies
- Language Arts/ English

Word of the week :　　　　　　　　　　　　　　　　　　　　　Due Date

	THURSDAY
Religion	
Reading	
Science	
Math	
Social Studies	
Language Arts/ English	

	FRIDAY
Religion	
Reading	
Science	
Math	
Social Studies	
Language Arts/ English	

Reminders:

1. _____

2. _____

3. _____

Note from parent to teacher _____
_____
_____

Note from teacher to parent _____

✢ *Thank You, God, for all Your help this year.*

 Daily Schedule

Time	Monday	Tuesday	Wednesday	Thursday	Friday

Special duties _____

Time	Monday	Tuesday	Wednesday	Thursday	Friday

Special duties _____

Notes

 **Notes**